Did

NO

A MISCELLANY

C000003530

Compiled by Julia Skinner

With particular reference to the work of Martin Andrew,
Bryan Howling, Frank Meeres, Barry Pardue, Adrian G Parker,
Elizabeth Purdy, Terence Sackett, Neil Storey, and Clive Tully.

THE FRANCIS FRITH COLLECTION

www.francisfrith.com

First published in the United Kingdom in 2010 by The Francis Frith Collection®

This edition published exclusively for Bradwell Books in 2012
For trade enquiries see: www.bradwellbooks.com or tel: 0800 834 920
ISBN 978-1-84589-530-3

Text and Design copyright The Francis Frith Collection®
Photographs copyright The Francis Frith Collection® except where indicated.

The Frith® photographs and the Frith® logo are reproduced under licence from
Heritage Photographic Resources Ltd, the owners of the Frith® archive and trademarks.
'The Francis Frith Collection', 'Francis Frith' and 'Frith' are registered trademarks of
Heritage Photographic Resources Ltd.

British Library Cataloguing in Publication Data

Did You Know? Norfolk - A Miscellany
Compiled by Julia Skinner
With particular reference to the work of Martin Andrew, Bryan Howling, Frank Meeres, Barry
Pardue, Adrian G Parker, Elizabeth Purdy, Terence Sackett, Neil Storey, and Clive Tully.

The Francis Frith Collection
Oakley Business Park,
Wylye Road, Dinton,
Wiltshire SP3 5EU
Tel: +44 (0) 1722 716 376
Email: info@francisfrith.co.uk
www.francisfrith.com

Printed and bound in Malaysia
Contains material sourced from responsibly managed forests

Front Cover: **THE BROADS, HUNSETT MILL ON RIVER ANT AT STALHAM c1925**
T213064p

The colour-tinting is for illustrative purposes only, and is not intended to be historically accurate

CONTENTS

2 Introduction

6 Norfolk Dialect Words and Phrases

8 Haunted Norfolk

10 Norfolk Miscellany

44 Sporting Norfolk

46 Quiz Questions

48 Recipes

52 Quiz Answers

54 Francis Frith - Pioneer Victorian Photographer

INTRODUCTION

Norfolk is made up of two distinct regions. Its first is a varied region of bare sandy heathlands in the west, marshlands and reedbeds in the east, and broad agricultural lands between, studded with remote and picturesque villages. Its second, more celebrated, region is to be found at its margins, where miles of wind-blown coastline are swept by the relentless waves of the North Sea.

Norfolk has a rich seafaring heritage. Since medieval times, its great harbours at King's Lynn and Great Yarmouth have been the haunt of fishermen following the herring and gathering lobsters and shellfish in its quieter coastal waters. For many hundreds of years coastal trading vessels have wound their way down the county's waterways to offload freight from the Low Countries, and these trading links are reflected in a Dutch influence on the architecture of houses in many of Norfolk's towns and villages. Many of Norfolk's ancient ports have now long since silted up, but have discovered new roles as popular resort towns, such as Cromer, Sheringham, Wells-next-the-Sea and Hunstanton, which are thronged with visitors in the summer months. Behind their crumbling cliffs are wide, solitary marshes, some now drained and cultivated, and rich in bird life.

Norfolk is almost an island: two sides are bordered by the North Sea, while the western boundary runs virtually beside the River Great Ouse, which flows into the Wash at King's Lynn. Only a few yards from the Ouse is the source of the Waveney, which flows eastwards forming the boundary with Suffolk and coming out into the sea at Great Yarmouth. The west of Norfolk south of King's Lynn is fenland, and the marshes were virtually impassable before the Romans began to drain them. The dykes fell into disrepair when the Roman legions departed in the fifth century; Norfolk again became isolated, until 18th-century engineers initiated a massive system of drains and sluices which nowadays controls the flow of water as far as the Midlands and the London area.

Villages in Norfolk grew out of settlements wherever a living could be made, and are usually sited on locally high ground and near water. Many developed along a droving lane which has become a main highway. These linear villages, such as Long Stratton, Horsford and Watton, usually have a wide main street, a relic of the days when cattle and sheep were driven through. However, the most important transport links in the county were by water. Goods from Europe were off-loaded at Great Yarmouth and put onto wherries, the flat-bottomed, broad-beamed boats with black sails that are often seen in pictures of Norfolk life. The main trade was up the Yare to Norwich, but the other rivers were busy too. Where the rivers were too shallow, they began to be canalised, allowing wherries to travel further upstream.

The first railway in Norfolk ran from Yarmouth to Norwich, opening in 1844, and over the next 50 years the railway reached every town in Norfolk and many villages too – at the peak of the railway age there were over 150 stations in the county. Trains took Norfolk produce such as turkeys and herrings to London, and also opened up the county to visitors from the cities, developing the holiday trade on which Norfolk has increasingly come to depend.

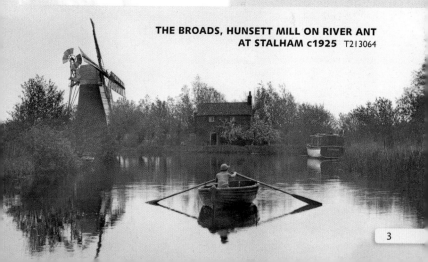

THE BROADS, HUNSETT MILL ON RIVER ANT AT STALHAM c1925 T213064

CROMER, THE SANDS 1899 44482

NORFOLK DIALECT WORDS AND PHRASES

'Afront' – in front.

'Ahind' – behind.

'Atwin' – between.

'Bishy barney bee' – a ladybird.

'Dodman' – a snail.

'Dudder' – to shiver.

'Dwile' – a floor cloth.

'Harnser' – a heron.

'I'll get wrong!' – I'll get told off!

'Lollop' – to move along slowly.

'Luggy' – deaf.

'Lummox' – a clumsy or awkward person.

'Mardle' – to gossip or chat.

'Mavish' – a thrush.

'Mawkin' – a scarecrow.

'Mawther' – a young woman.

'On the huh' – slanted, not level or straight.

'Squit' – talking nonsense.

'Titty-totty' – very small.

'Uhmtie-tump' – a mole hill.

'Warmint' – vermin, or a varmint, a troublesome person.

RANWORTH, THE STAITHE c1945 R9047

HAUNTED NORFOLK

In the Middle Ages, Queen Isabella conspired with her lover to murder her husband, Edward II. When her son became king, Edward III, he had his mother imprisoned in Castle Rising near King's Lynn for some time. It is said that she went mad there, and her ghostly shrieks can be heard around the castle walls at night. A local tale says that Castle Rising is linked with Red Mount Chapel in St James Park in King's Lynn via a secret haunted tunnel. A drunken fiddler decided to explore the tunnel, taking his dog with him, and was never seen again, but the sound of ghostly fiddle music can be heard in the area, as well as the whimpering of his dog, desperate to get out of the tunnel.

A mysterious grey lady is said to haunt Augustine Steward House at Tombland in Norwich, formerly a medieval merchant's trading house. She is reputed to be the ghost of a young woman who died there after the townspeople boarded up the house during a plague epidemic; unbeknown to them, she had survived the plague which had killed the other occupants of the house, but she starved to death, unable to get out.

Several villages in Norfolk are said to be haunted by a phantom black dog known as 'Old Shuck', and a sighting of the hound presages death – in fact, an old East Anglian saying when someone was dying was 'the Black Dog is at his heels'.

The bridge at Potter Heigham is one of the few medieval bridges surviving on the Broadland rivers, and is said to be haunted by a phantom coach and four which is driven by the Devil; it appears at midnight and plunges from the bridge into the water below.

The Hippodrome Circus building in Great Yarmouth, on the junction of St Peter's Road and St George's Road, is one of only two surviving custom-built circus buildings in Britain (the other is in Blackpool). The building is reputed to be haunted by several ghosts. One is the shade of George Gilbert, the circus showman who built the Hippodrome in 1903. The other is known as 'Swinging Billy', the ghost of a former circus worker who hanged himself inside the building.

CASTLE RISING, 1898 40895

NORFOLK MISCELLANY

In the Middle Ages, Norfolk was one of the richest and most densely-populated parts of England. This wealth was based on wool, but Norfolk's importance in the wool trade declined in the 18th century as watermills in Yorkshire and Lancashire harnessed the power of fast-flowing streams to drive the newly-invented machinery in their textile mills: the slow-moving streams and rivers of Norfolk were unsuitable for this purpose, and Norfolk's once great woollen and weaving industry, where the village of Worstead gave its name to fine cloth, came to an end.

The Anglo-Saxon name for Norwich was 'Norwic', meaning 'the north settlement' or 'the north trading port'. The Vikings ruled Norwich from AD870-917, and left their mark in several street names, such as Fishergate, the street where the fishermen lived, and Westlegate, the street where wassal (white bread) was sold. Some of Norwich's other street names reflect the goods sold in its markets in the Middle Ages: wood at Timberhill, hay on the Haymarket, pigs at Hog Hill and horses at Horsefair, off St Faith's Lane.

After the Norman Conquest in 1066, control over Norwich was established by the new rulers with the erection of one of the earliest motte and bailey castles in England, at the highest spot in the town. A stone keep was built by Henry I, but the one seen in photograph 28177 (opposite) is the result of much subsequent rebuilding. It has been used as a prison in the past, but is now the Norwich Castle Museum and Art Gallery.

In 1549 'Kett's Rebellion' broke out in Norwich, an outburst of non-violent protest led by Robert Kett of Wymondham. Several thousand people gathered on Mousehold Heath, but were crushed by Swiss mercenaries under the Earl of Warwick; Kett was captured and hanged from the keep of Norwich Castle. The authorities ordered a local holiday to be established celebrating Kett's downfall, and for all the city shops to close on 27th August 'from henceforward forever'! But attitudes have changed over the years, and on the 400th anniversary of Kett's death a plaque was put up at the castle in his memory.

NORWICH, THE CATTLE MARKET AND CASTLE 1891 28177

11

The foundation stone for Norwich Cathedral was laid in 1096, and the building is still essentially Norman, but its great spire is late 15th-century. Its predecessor had been blown through the choir roof in a great gale in 1362; this also resulted in the building of the superb spacious clerestory of the choir. The most successful and harmonious change to the Norman cathedral at Norwich over the years was the addition of stone vaults throughout, after a fire in 1463 when the cathedral was struck by lightning. The intricate rib patterns and their glorious carved bosses complement the Norman work of 300 years before, the shafts and columns leading the eye up to the vaulted roof. This is one of the masterpieces of medieval English architecture (see photograph 28152, below).

NORWICH, CATHEDRAL, CHOIR WEST 1891 28152

NORWICH, MARKET PLACE 1929 81796

During the Middle Ages one of the most important medieval English religious mystics was Julian of Norwich, an anchorite (a hermit living in a cell attached to the church, who engaged in contemplative prayer) at St Julian's Church on King Street in the city. Her major work was 'Revelations of Divine Love' (or 'A Revelation of Love – in Sixteen Shewings), believed to be the first book written in English by a woman. Her saying 'All shall be well and all shall be well and all manner of thing shall be well' is still one of the most famous lines in Catholic theological writing.

Photograph 81796 (above) shows Norwich's market place full of noise and colour on market day. In the background is the tower of the 15th-century church of St Peter Mancroft, which is the resting place of Sir Thomas Browne, the 17th-century religious thinker and physician who campaigned to have cremation recognised as a legal form of burial; his 'Urn Burial' and 'Religio Medici' are acknowledged prose masterpieces.

In 1566, 30 master craftsmen from Europe were invited to come to Norwich to reinvigorate its declining weaving trade; 24 were Dutch and six were Walloons, a French-speaking people from what is now Belgium. Soon over 4,000 of their countrymen had joined them in the city. These immigrants, known locally as 'Strangers', brought many things to Norwich, including banknotes, tulips and their favourite pet, the canary, a bird now so closely associated with the city that Norwich City Football Club play in canary yellow colours, and are nicknamed 'The Canaries'. Over the years, local breeders have established a specific type of these delightful little birds, known as the Norwich Canary.

By the 18th century, shoemaking was a burgeoning local industry in Norwich. James Smith, who had a leather shop in the city for 40 years, had a 'cunning scheme' in the 1790s: he is said to have been the first person in the world to think of selling boots and shoes in stock sizes, rather than having each customer individually measured.

Millions of years ago Norfolk was at the bottom of the North Sea. It was then that the county's chalk beds were laid down, which contained nodules of silicon – flint. Flint is exceptionally hard, and for centuries was used by Norfolk people as their traditional building material. It can be used as whole flints, with their white surface, or the flints can be cut in half, producing a very dark appearance. They can even be cut into little squares and used to infill limestone or chalk to create delicate patterns known as flushwork.

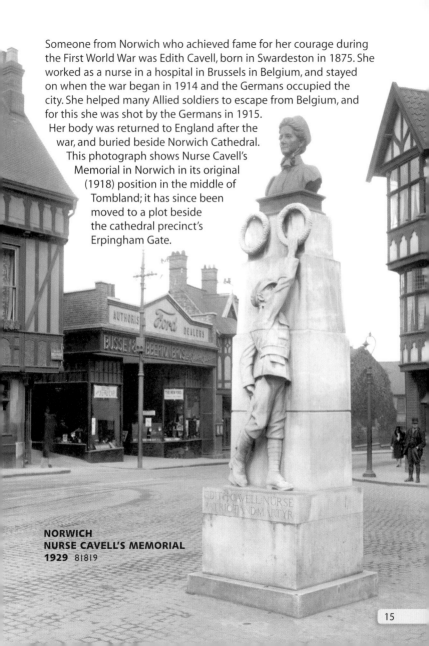

Someone from Norwich who achieved fame for her courage during the First World War was Edith Cavell, born in Swardeston in 1875. She worked as a nurse in a hospital in Brussels in Belgium, and stayed on when the war began in 1914 and the Germans occupied the city. She helped many Allied soldiers to escape from Belgium, and for this she was shot by the Germans in 1915.

Her body was returned to England after the war, and buried beside Norwich Cathedral.

This photograph shows Nurse Cavell's Memorial in Norwich in its original (1918) position in the middle of Tombland; it has since been moved to a plot beside the cathedral precinct's Erpingham Gate.

NORWICH
NURSE CAVELL'S MEMORIAL
1929 81819

A distinguishing characteristic of over 100 Norfolk churches is a round tower, often made of flint. Photograph B496004 (right) of the church at Bradwell shows an excellent example of such a round tower – but no one really knows why they were built this way.

**BRADWELL,
THE CHURCH
c1955** B496004

The market town of Swaffham, with its Queen Anne and Georgian buildings, was once hailed as 'the Montpellier of England'. Swaffham's parish church of St Peter and St Paul is a magnificent Perpendicular edifice with a grand hammerbeam roof and delicate spire. Tradition says that the church was built at the expense of the 'Swaffham pedlar', John Chapman, who found two pots of gold in his garden after being guided to them in a dream. There is a delightful wooden carving of him on the prayer desk inside the church.

Photograph 42760 (below) shows Church Street in East Dereham in 1898. This lovely street leads down to the church where the poet William Cowper was laid to rest after his death in 1800. The first Christian settlement at Dereham is said to have been a nunnery established in AD654 by St Withburga, daughter of King Anna of the East Anglians.

The medieval town of Diss prospered as a market for cloth and linen thread, which was spun and woven from locally-grown flax. The spacious market place at Diss is dominated by St Mary's Church with its Norman tower, 14th-century arcades, impressive clerestory, and knapped flint chancel. For many years the rector here was the poet laureate John Skelton, who was also a tutor to Henry VIII when he was Prince of Wales.

EAST DEREHAM, CHURCH STREET 1898 42760

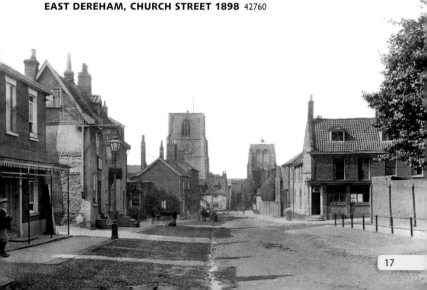

COLTISHALL, A CORNFIELD 1902 48127

In previous centuries Norfolk was overrun with rabbits. When farm workers 'lived in' on the farms, rabbits formed a large part of their diet and were known as 'hollow meat'. In fact, some farmworkers in the county got so bored of eating rabbit that a proviso had to be made that they should only be fed 'hollow meat' for a certain number of days a week.

The scene in photograph 48127 (above) is a reminder of what arable farming in Norfolk used to look like. Sheaves of wheat are heaped in wind-blown stooks to dry in the field, traditionally left there 'for 2 church bells', ie the church bells ringing for two Sunday services, between ten to fourteen days, depending on when the crop was cut.

The Guildhall at Thetford holds a collection of 100 portraits of members of great East Anglian families, bequeathed by the antiquary Prince Frederick Duleep Singh. The radical writer and activist, Thomas Paine, author of the influential 'The Rights of Man' and a participant in both the American and French revolutions, was born in Thetford in 1737 and educated at the Free Grammar School in the town.

Great Yarmouth lies at the mouth of the River Yare. In the Middle Ages it developed into a thriving port, but the river mouth continually choked up with sand. All attempts to create harbour entrances that would not silt up were unsuccessful until 1560, when the seventh attempt saw a Dutch expert brought in to supervise the building of a new cut, this time stabilised by wooden piling. It worked, and survives to this day as the harbour entrance. Great Yarmouth's holiday industry really began in the mid 19th century, when it became the first Norfolk coastal town to obtain a railway link, and soon the Wellington Pier and Britannia Pier were stretching their promenades out to sea; a tradition of entertainment, attractions and ornamental gardens was begun in the town, and Great Yarmouth remains Norfolk's biggest and most popular coastal resort.

The earliest known document to call the town Great Yarmouth comes from the reign of Edward I (1272-1307). It was called Great Yarmouth to distinguish it from Little Yarmouth on the other side of the river, now Southtown, and not (as is often thought) from Yarmouth on the Isle of Wight.

GREAT YARMOUTH, BRITANNIA PIER 1904 52337

GREAT YARMOUTH, THE HARBOUR c1900 G56510

Although the port of Great Yarmouth was thriving in the Middle Ages, the town's prosperity was founded on herring fishing. The fishing industry reached its height in the 19th century, and during the season, about ten weeks from the end of September, the town's population would be swelled by thousands of fishermen with their wives and daughters, who gutted and packed the fish. Herrings were also dried and cured into the famous Yarmouth bloaters. The fishing industry continued during the first half of the 20th century, when sailing boats were superseded by steam drifters, but by the 1950s fish stocks were depleted, and it came to an end. Its herring fleet is now gone, but Great Yarmouth's fishing heritage is commemorated in the Time and Tide museum on Blackfriar's Road, housed in a former herring smokery.

The Fishermen's Hospital at Great Yarmouth is shown in photograph 19896, below. It is a series of 20 small cottages, each with one room downstairs and a bedroom built into the roof. The hospital was founded in 1702 and could accommodate up to twenty former fishermen, who were either disabled or over 60 years old, and their wives. However, if a fisherman died, his widow had to leave the hospital – unless she could persuade one of the other fishermen there to marry her!

Great Yarmouth's parish church of St Nicholas was damaged by bombing in the Second World War. When it was rebuilt it was given a neo-Gothic interior with broad aisles, but the funds for the church's rebuilding could not stretch to a replacement spire. The now-lost spire of the church can be seen in the background of photograph 19896, below.

**GREAT YARMOUTH, THE FISHERMEN'S HOSPITAL
1896** 19896

King Street in Great Yarmouth was so-named after Charles II visited the town in 1671. St George's Church in King Street is one of the few Classical-style churches in East Anglia (photograph 28723, below). It was built in 1714, modelled on a baroque design borrowed from Christopher Wren. This historic church, now used as an arts centre, has characteristic 18th-century galleries, pulpit and reredos, and a plaster ceiling above the nave.

Great Yarmouth suffered much damage from air raids during the Second World War, including the destruction of many of the town's historic Rows. These were 156 parallel narrow alleyways which ran between the Market Place and King Street on one side, and the Quays along the river on the other. They developed in this way in medieval times, as houses were crammed close together within the town walls. Special carts called 'trolls' were developed to negotiate the narrow Rows – there is a modern replica of one outside Great Yarmouth's Town Hall. The Rows all had names, many taken from nearby inns, and were also given numbers in 1804 to avoid confusion. One was named Snatchbody Row, after the bodysnatcher Thomas Vaughan who lived there in the 19th century. He rented a room in a house in Row 6, where he secretly kept bodies that he had dug out of St Nicholas's churchyard after they had been buried, prior to sending them to London where he sold them to anatomy students.

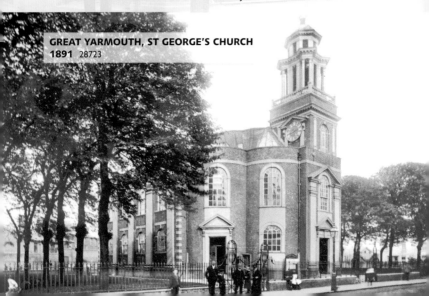

GREAT YARMOUTH, ST GEORGE'S CHURCH
1891 28723

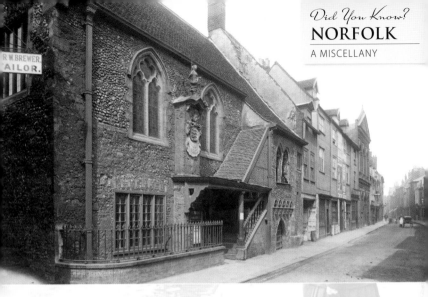

GREAT YARMOUTH, THE TOLHOUSE 1891 28703

Photograph 28703 (above) shows the historic flint-built Tolhouse in Great Yarmouth, which at the time of this photograph was used as the town's free library, but is now a museum. Built in the 13th century, it served as Great Yarmouth's town hall, court and gaol for 600 years, and is the oldest surviving civic building in England. In 1645 the Corporation of Great Yarmouth sent for Matthew Hopkins, James I's infamous Witchfinder General, to investigate sixteen local women accused of being witches; five were condemned to death, and were held in the dungeon of the Tolhouse before their execution. The grated dungeon window can be seen at street level.

In photograph 37959 on page 53 of Regent Road in Great Yarmouth, one of the youths is holding a goat harnessed to a small cart, which would have been used for giving children rides on the beach. Goat carriages were a popular form of children's amusement in the town in the 19th century, but animal lovers objected to them and they were banned by the Borough Council in 1911 – although the goat in this photograph looks happy enough.

23

The naval hero Lord Nelson was a Norfolk man, born in Burnham Thorpe in 1758, and a road, a court, a terrace and a square in Great Yarmouth are named after his most famous battle, at Trafalgar in 1805. The town also celebrates his life in the Norfolk Nelson Museum on South Quay. After Nelson's death, Great Yarmouth was chosen as the place for a Norfolk memorial to him, sited on the coast in the South Denes. The 144ft-tall monument, topped by a figure of Britannia, is known as the Nelson Monument, but its correct name is the Norfolk Naval Pillar. A local legend says that the architect of the monument jumped to his death from the top in despair when he realised that the figure of Britannia was facing the 'wrong' way, looking inland rather than out to sea; in fact, Britannia was designed to face this way, looking towards Nelson's birthplace on the north Norfolk coast.

HORNING, ON THE BROADS 1902 48108

South of Great Yarmouth is South Denes. In the mid 19th century there was a hospital here where sailors who were mentally ill were sent for treatment. Thus the phrase 'Going to Yarmouth' became naval slang for someone showing signs of mental strain.

The Lifeboat Memorial at Caister-on-Sea commemorates the deaths of nine lifeboat crewmen in a great storm in 1901 whilst on a rescue mission. At the enquiry afterwards, the surviving crewmen were asked why they had carried on when conditions made a rescue impossible. They famously answered: 'Caister men never turn back.'

Caister-on-Sea is now a popular modern seaside resort, but it has a historic castle, built in the 1440s by Sir John Fastolf, an English knight who fought in the Hundred Years War; he is believed to have been the inspiration for the character of Falstaff in several of Shakespeare's plays. The castle later passed to the Paston family, and its chequered history features in the famous 'Paston Letters', a unique collection of the correspondence of a Norfolk family during the turbulent period of the 15th century.

The gaff-rigged wherry was precisely designed for Broadland conditions, and fleets of them once plied the waterways between Great Yarmouth and Norwich. An example of a wherry is seen in photograph 48108, opposite, with its traditional black sail. The wherrymen were the prime movers in the past of grain, coal, timber, harvested reeds, crops and manufactured goods throughout Broadland and to the coastal ports.

The Benedictine Abbey of St Benet-at-Holm was founded in 1020 by King Canute, but little remains of the abbey now except its gateway, which is a well-known landmark on the bank of the lower Bure. The Bishop of Norwich holds a service at the abbey ruins each August, traditionally arriving by river on a wherry.

The Norfolk Broads have been a watery playground for holidaymakers for decades, but these expanses of smooth water are actually man-made. In medieval times peat was dug here on a grand scale; the huge diggings were prone to flooding, and were inundated during periods of rising water levels, resulting in the landscape we see today. The capital of the Broads is Wroxham, and it is a popular starting point for boating. A bridge over the Bure divides the mainly residential area of Wroxham to the west and the village of Hoveton on the east side of the river. In photograph 70890 (below) we are looking from Hoveton towards the bridge leading to Wroxham.

HOVETON, THE VILLAGE 1921 70890

POTTER HEIGHAM, THE BRIDGE 1934 86381

The bridge at Potter Heigham is seen in photograph 86381 (above), where the warning sign – 'Caution, proceed slowly' – says it all. The bridge has headroom of only six feet at high tide, and sails and masts have to be lowered to allow river craft to pass under the bridge, then raised again on the other side. It was a matter of pride amongst traditional boatmen – and required great skill – to approach the bridge at full speed, reef the sail, lower the mast and emerge the other side without losing way.

The church at the Broadland village of Acle is unusual because it has a thatched nave roof and an octagonal top to its round tower. It also contains an inscription written on the wall plaster of the chancel in the 15th century, describing an outbreak of plague in the area: 'the brute beast plague raged hour by hour'.

Photograph S473016 (right) shows the corn windmill at Sutton, nine floors high and reputed to be the tallest in Norfolk. The boat-shaped cap is characteristic of Norfolk mills.

**SUTTON,
THE WINDMILL
c1955** S473016

The names of several villages in east Norfolk end in '-by', such as Hemsby, indicating that they were founded by the Vikings, as '-by' is an old Norse word for 'town'. Most of them are in the area known as Flegg, itself a Viking word for a marshy place.

One of the most beautiful of the Broads churches is St Helen's at Ranworth. The mid 15th-century rood screen inside the church (photograph 86391, below) is one of the finest in the country, and restoration has revealed beautifully coloured portraits of apostles and saints.

The major industry of Fakenham in the 19th and 20th centuries was printing, and this heritage is recalled in an unusual way: a number of printing blocks have been set into the surface of the town's market place. The town is also home to a unique museum, the Fakenham Museum of Gas and Local History, which is based in the only surviving town gasworks in England and has displays of all kinds of lighting, heating, cooking and domestic gas equipment from the past.

RANWORTH, THE CHURCH ROOD SCREEN 1934 86391

HOLT 1922 72563

Holt, between Fakenham and Cromer, boasts a wealth of Georgian houses huddled haphazardly around the market place, which was rebuilt all of a piece after a town fire in 1708. One of Holt's curiosities is the Pineapple Obelisk, inscribed with the mileage to Norfolk's principal towns from Melton Constable Hall where it originally served as a gatepost – but incorrect information for the distances from Holt, where it now stands!

The most famous inhabitant of the seaside village of West Runton, near Cromer, died some 600,000 years ago: a giant elephant, whose skeleton was found in the cliffs after erosion in the 1990s. It is the most complete such skeleton in the world, and is on display at Norwich Castle Museum.

Cromer developed as a seaside resort in the early 19th century and is mentioned as a bathing place in Jane Austen's 'Emma', but the town really burgeoned into a popular resort on Norfolk's north coast with the coming of the railways. The 160ft tower of the mainly Perpendicular church of St Peter and St Paul at Cromer soars majestically over the town and is a prominent day mark for shipping in the coastal waters. The tower once acted as a lighthouse and is the second loftiest in Norfolk after that of Norwich Cathedral.

Cromer Pier is often advertised as being the only place in England from which one can watch the sun both rise and set over the sea.

Norfolk's lifeboatmen are renowned for their courage. Photograph 72651 (below) shows the crew of the lifeboat 'Louisa Heartwell' at Cromer in 1922. Henry Blogg, the coxswain of the 'Louisa Heartwell' from 1909 to 1947, was the most decorated lifeboatman in Britain, earning three gold and four silver medals, the George Cross and the British Empire medal for his bravery. Other crew members in this photograph are also proudly displaying their medals.

CROMER, THE LIFEBOAT 1922 72651

SHERINGHAM, FISHERMEN 1893 33313

The town of Sheringham comprises two villages, Upper and Lower Sheringham. The Church of All Saints at Upper Sheringham is mainly 14th-century, and contains several fine tombs of the Upcher family. The bench ends in the church are remarkable; the decorative carvings depict a baby in swaddling clothes, Nebuchadnezzar eating grass, and even a mermaid, which is said to have been modelled from life from a mermaid who would creep ashore and listen to the congregation singing from the north door.

Sheringham fishermen ventured out in open boats in all weathers, pursuing crabs, lobsters, herring, cod and whiting. Proud and independent, they shared not just their perilous profession but also their religion – most were devout Salvationists. They were the traditional enemies of Cromer men, who disparagingly referred to fishermen born of parents local to the town as 'Shannocks' – this may derive from 'shanny', a dialect word meaning 'unruly.'

The parish church of St Nicholas at Blakeney is unusual for having two towers, one at each end. Blakeney was a major port when the church was built, with its ships trading as far away as Iceland, and the smaller tower of the church used to carry a beacon at night which served as a mark for sailors heading for the port.

Norfolk has several links with the Native American princess Pocahontas, famous for saving the life of Captain John Smith during the early settlement of the American colony of Virginia, by throwing herself over his body to prevent him being clubbed to death by her father's warriors. As a young lad, Captain Smith worked in King's Lynn as a merchant's apprentice. Heacham was once the home of John Rolfe (1585-1622), another Virginian settler, who married Pocahontas in 1614. The couple came to England for a visit, staying at Heacham Hall, and Pocahontas was presented at court to James I. She died as she was returning to Virginia, at Gravesend, and was buried there, but there is an alabaster memorial to her in St Mary's Church in Heacham. John Rolfe and Pocahontas had one child, their son Thomas. Thomas Rolfe's daughter with his first wife, Anne, was brought up in England and married Peter Elwin of Thurning in Norfolk; Thomas married again in America and had more children. One of the descendants of the union between John Rolfe and Pocahontas is Nancy Reagan, former First Lady of the United States.

WELLS-NEXT-THE-SEA, THE QUAY 1929 81998

Wells-next-the-Sea was a port long ago, but from Wells-next-the-Sea to Blakeney a great sand barrier holds back all but the most vicious tides, and the quay at Wells is now stranded a mile from the open sea. Photograph 81998 (above) shows whelk boats arriving at the quay with their catch in 1929. The Wells whelkers were renowned along this coast for their persistence in pursuing their trade. Dropping pots from open clinker-built boats in foul weather meant that whelkers could often find themselves stranded for hours on end on the wrong side of the bar, waiting for the tide. The parish register for Wells-next-the-Sea for 1583 records the loss of a Wells ship coming back from Spain off the west coast of England. Fourteen sailors were drowned in the wreck, which was blamed on a curse laid on the ship by a witch from King's Lynn.

Walsingham was a major centre of pilgrimage in the Middle Ages. Pilgrims came to see the Holy House, a miraculous re-creation in the grounds of Walsingham Priory of the house in Nazareth where Jesus was brought up, together with other wonders. The shrine at Walsingham was destroyed when the priory was dissolved in 1538. In 1897 the 14th-century Slipper Chapel at Walsingham was re-established as a Roman Catholic shrine, the National Shrine of Our Lady of Walsingham, and in the 20th century an Anglican Shrine of Our Lady of Walsingham was also established in the town. Walsingham is once again a place of peace to pilgrims who come to worship there.

The Slipper Chapel at Walsingham is so-named because in medieval times this was where pilgrims would remove their shoes before walking barefoot for the last Holy Mile to the shrine of Our Lady at Walsingham.

HOLKHAM HALL 1922 72639

SNETTISHAM

SNETTISHAM, VILLAGE SIGN c1960 S464022

The circular object at the top of the village sign for Snettisham seen in photograph S464022 (left) represents a Celtic torc, or neck ornament. A fabulous collection of more than 100 gold, silver and electrum torcs from the Iron Age was found here, known as the Snettisham Hoard. The torcs are now in Norwich Castle Museum.

Holkham Hall in Norfolk was built in the 18th century to a design by Palladio (photograph 72639, opposite). Within the entrance hall are beautiful statues, one of which, of the goddess Diana, is notable for its depiction of classical drapery. The house and estate was inherited by Thomas William Coke (1754-1842), 'Coke of Norfolk', who was famous for his pioneering methods of agriculture, animal husbandry and livestock breeding and is recognised as one of the instigators of the Agricultural Revolution in Britain. Many of his agricultural experiments took place on the Holkham estate.

Marsh Samphire, or glasswort, grows on salt marshes around the Norfolk coast, and the green fleshy tips can be eaten. Samphire is often known as 'poor man's asparagus', but is also enjoyed by the rich – it was served at the royal wedding breakfast of Prince Charles and Lady Diana Spencer in 1981, as a symbol of the royal residence of Sandringham in Norfolk, where the royal family gathers to celebrate Christmas each year.

Norfolk is renowned for the quality of its turkeys. In the 17th century flocks of the famous Norfolk Black turkeys were driven on foot from Norfolk to London for the Christmas markets, in great droves of 500 birds or more. The journey took about 3 months, and the birds would have their feet coated in tar to protect them on the journey. Daniel Defoe recorded in the early 18th century that each year 300 droves of Norfolk turkeys went through the town of Stratford St Mary in Suffolk on their way to London.

KING'S LYNN, HIGH STREET 1908 60023

The sublime town of King's Lynn is on the east bank of the River Ouse, two miles from the Wash. An early industry in the area was salt production, and in Anglo-Saxon times there were fifty salt pans operating. King's Lynn flourished into one of the richest ports in the land in medieval times. Cargoes of wool, cloth from Flanders, and timber from the Baltic crossed into England here. From the 16th century more merchants and traders came into Lynn, and a huge manufacturing industry developed, including textiles, weaving, tanning, milling, baking, shoemaking, shipbuilding, ropemaking and goldsmithing. Silting of the Ouse's ponderous waters in later centuries robbed the town of much of its former prestige as a seaport, but its many graceful buildings have brought to it the appellation of 'most romantic town in England'.

King's Lynn was not always the name of the town. Founded by Herbert, Bishop of Norwich, around 1100, it was known as Bishop's Lynn until it passed from the Church to the Crown during the reign of Henry VIII.

It is said that the mark of the Devil's hoofprint can be seen in Devil's Alley at King's Lynn. According to legend, the Devil arrived by ship and went ashore to gather some souls. A local priest followed him to this alley, and used prayers and holy water to drive the Devil away. The Devil was so annoyed at being foiled in his plan that he stamped his foot on the ground before leaving, and the imprint can still be seen.

St Nicholas's Chapel in King's Lynn, just off Tuesday Market Place, has an unusual 'angel roof' dating from c1400. The angels are on projecting struts over each window head; all are depicted full length with spread wings, and are unconnected to the roof. Each angel is different, with many either holding or playing a musical instrument.

KING'S LYNN, TUESDAY MARKET PLACE 1898 40886

During the Civil War King's Lynn was held for the king, and was besieged by Parliamentary forces for almost three weeks before surrendering. During the siege a 16lb cannonball went through a window of St Margaret's Church and damaged a pillar. The cannonball can now be seen suspended from the roof at the entrance to Hampton Court in Nelson Street.

Many British towns suffered air raids during the Second World War, but only a few places experienced them in the First World War, and two Norfolk towns were among them. Great Yarmouth and King's Lynn were the first towns in the country to be attacked by a German Zeppelin airship during the war, when they suffered an aerial bombardment in January 1915.

The reason why there is a road in King's Lynn named after the American president John F Kennedy is that an American firm, Dow Agro-chemicals, opened a plant in the town just after Kennedy had been elected President in 1960.

The city of Vancouver on Canada's Pacific coast, and another Vancouver, in the nearby US state of Washington, are both named after Captain George Vancouver RN of King's Lynn, who undertook surveying voyages of the Pacific northwest coast, sent by the Admiralty in the 1790s to prepare navigation charts from the Columbia river to Alaska. A statue of him was erected in his hometown in 2000, beside the Custom House where his father John Jasper Vancouver was Deputy Collector (see photograph K28717, opposite).

KING'S LYNN, THE CUSTOM HOUSE AND THE VANCOUVER STATUE 2003 K28717

The beautiful Custom House at King's Lynn was built in the Palladian style in the 1680s (see photograph K28717, above). Originally intended as an Exchange for local merchants, it became the Custom House in the early 18th century. This Renaissance gem has come to symbolise Lynn, and is now the tourist information centre.

SPORTING NORFOLK

Georgian Norwich was renowned for its bare-knuckle fighters, but perhaps the most famous fighter of all from the city was Jem Mace, landlord of the Swan Tavern which used to stand in Swan Lane (where there is a plaque to him), who was the bare-knuckle boxing champion of the world. He became the world-champion bare-knuckle fighter for the first time in 1862 when he fought Tom King, a man almost twice his size. The fight lasted 43 rounds, and by the end Mace's right arm was damaged and he could only fight using his left arm. In 1870 Jem Mace travelled to America to fight Tom Allen for the world-champion title in a suburb of New Orleans. The prize was 10,000 dollars and Mace won in the tenth round.

Norwich City Football Club was formed in 1902. City's best years came in the early 1990s under the management of Mike – 'St Michael' – Walker. Norwich City were founder members of the Premier League in 1992-93 and contenders for the first ever Premier League title, eventually finishing third and qualifying for Europe for the first time. One of the finest goals in football history was scored at Carrow Road by Justin Fashanu against Liverpool in 1980, voted the BBC Match of the Day goal of the season. The nickname of Norwich City Football Club was originally 'The Cits' (short for 'Citizens'), but the current nickname of 'The Canaries' seems to have come into use during the 1906-07 season, probably a reference to the canary rearing that Norwich was famous for. When City played in their new strip of yellow shirts for the first time in the following season, one local newspaper marked the event with the comment 'The Cits are dead, but the Canaries are very much alive'.

Great Yarmouth has an important and popular horseracing course with high quality racing, attracting top trainers and jockeys. The annual Eastern Festival is a highlight in the local calendar, with 3 days of flat racing. The first racecourse at Great Yarmouth was built on the Denes in 1810, where officers from the military barracks could race and exercise their horses, but the current racecourse is at Jellicoe Road. The new Lord Nelson Grandstand was opened in 2004.

Great Yarmouth Town Football Club was established in 1897. The club's nickname is 'The Bloaters', after the famous Yarmouth bloaters produced in the town. One of the club's most impressive seasons was 1926-27 – despite losing the first league game of the season, they went on to be undefeated in the remaining 23 games that year. Perhaps the club's finest hour was in the FA Cup tournament of the 1953-54 season when they pulled off one of the famous 'giant-killing' acts for which the FA Cup is famous, defeating Crystal Palace to reach the second round of the tournament.

A modern addition to Great Yarmouth's sporting facilities came in 2008, when the world's first Segway Grand Prix track was opened at the Pleasure Beach gardens. A Segway is a two-wheeled electric vehicle on which the rider balances as the vehicle moves along. The vehicle is steered by the rider leaning forward, backwards, and left or right, whilst using a tall steering handlebar.

King's Lynn has produced an England Test Cricketer, Peter Howard Parfitt, who attended King Edward VII Grammar School in the town. He played for Middlesex CCC between 1956 and 1972, captaining the 1st XI from 1968 to 1970. He played in 37 Tests for England between 1962 and 1972.

The King's Lynn Stars are the town's motorcycle speedway team. 2006 was a good year for The Stars, who not only won the Premier League Championship but also the Premier Trophy and the 2006 Premier Knock-out Cup. They almost repeated the treble in 2007, once again winning the Premier Trophy and Premier League Knock-out Cup, but lost the league championship in the play-off semi-final to the Sheffield Tigers, despite finishing top of the Premier League table. However, they became Treble Champions for the second time in 2009, the first club ever to have achieved this feat.

The golf links at Cromer became a full 18-hole course in 1895, and the famous course designer Tom Morris was involved in advising the club. It is considered by the famous British golfer Tony Jacklin to be one of the finest in the country, and was featured by him in a film of his favourite golf courses.

QUIZ QUESTIONS

Answers on page 52.

1. What is the connection between Norfolk and a famous fictional black horse?

2. Which Great Yarmouth MP put his name to a historic document that cost him his life?

3. What was the connection between Sir Robert Walpole, Britain's first Prime Minister, and King's Lynn?

4. Photograph 81810 (opposite) shows Samson and Hercules House at Tombland in Norwich, probably built by Christopher Jay, mayor of the city in 1657. The figures of Samson and Hercules graced the front of the house from Jay's time until 1789 when they were taken down, but they were replaced there in 1900. The figure on the right of the view is a copy of the original, whilst the figure on the left hand side is the same statue put there almost 350 years ago – but do you know which is Samson and which is Hercules?

5. What are 'Stookey Blues'?

6. What would you be doing in Norfolk if you were 'quanting'?

7. What is the connection between Norfolk and the pantomime story of 'The Babes in the Wood'?

8. What is Grimes' Graves, on the Breckland heath seven miles northwest of Thetford?

9. A famous fiery lady was a queen in the Norfolk area in the early years of the Roman occupation, and caused the invaders some problems. Who was she, and what was the name of the Celtic tribe that she ruled?

10. A word commonly found in Norfolk is a 'staithe' – what is this?

NORWICH, SAMSON AND HERCULES HOUSE, TOMBLAND 1929 81810

TEAS

RECIPE

NELSON SQUARES

This recipe recalls one of Norfolk's most famous sons, Admiral Lord Nelson, who was born at Burnham Thorpe near King's Lynn in 1758. A commemorative statue of Lord Nelson stands in the cathedral close at Norwich (photograph 88673, opposite). Replace the mixed peel with an extra 50g/2oz of dried fruit, if preferred.

> 225g/8oz stale white bread, with crusts removed
> 300ml/ ½ pint milk
> 115g/4oz currants or raisins, or a mixture of both
> 50g/2oz mixed peel, finely chopped
> 50g/2oz suet
> 50g/2oz demerara sugar
> 1-2 level teaspoonfuls mixed spice, to taste
> 1 egg for the mixture
> 500g/1lb shortcrust pastry or puff pastry
> 1 beaten egg or a little extra milk for sealing and glazing the pastry

Soak the bread in the milk for half an hour, then beat out any lumps to leave a smooth mixture. Add the dried fruit, mixed peel, suet, sugar and mixed spice and mix well. Mix in the egg, and add a little extra milk if the mixture is too stiff to spread easily.

Pre-heat the oven to 180°C/350°F/Gas Mark 4. Grease a deep 22cm (9 inch) square baking tin. Roll out the pastry and cut into two sections, making one approx 28cm (11 inches) square, and the other approx 22cm (9 inches) square. Use the bigger section to line the base of the baking tin – the pastry should come up the sides of the tin. Spread the fruit mixture evenly over the pastry in the tin, leaving a slight gap around the sides. Brush the edge of the pastry with some of the beaten egg or milk, cover the mixture with the other square of pastry and pinch the edges together with the bottom layer to seal them together and enclose the mixture. Brush the surface with milk or beaten egg and prick some holes in the surface with a fork. Bake in the oven for 1½ to 2 hours, until the pastry is golden brown. Leave to cool in the tin then turn out, sprinkle with sugar and cut into squares before serving.

NORWICH, LORD NELSON'S STATUE IN CATHEDRAL CLOSE 1938 88673x

RECIPE

HERRINGS WITH MUSTARD SAUCE

Great Yarmouth was once a major a centre of herring fishery. Photograph G56503 (opposite) shows the town's fish market c1900. After a good fishing trip, the drifters have unloaded their haul into baskets known as 'swills', specially made wicker baskets for herrings which were unique to Great Yarmouth and Lowestoft. On the wharf the bowler-hatted tellers are assessing the catch prior to its sale by auction. In this recipe, the herrings are served with a savoury stuffing for a tasty lunch or supper. The mustard sauce is a reminder of Norfolk's famous mustard industry – bright yellow fields of mustard have been grown in the county ever since Jeremiah Colman opened his first mustard mill near Norwich 1814 and started making his condiment.

> 4 large herrings
> 3 heaped tablespoonfuls fresh white breadcrumbs
> 1 heaped teaspoonful finely chopped parsley
> A squeeze of lemon juice
> Grated rind of half a lemon
> Salt and black pepper
> Oil for frying
> 25g/1oz butter
>
> For the mustard sauce:
> 40g/1½ oz butter
> 25g/1oz plain flour
> 450ml/ ¾ pint milk
> Salt and black pepper
> 1 level tablespoonful dry Norfolk mustard powder
> 1 tablespoonful wine vinegar
> 1 level teaspoonful caster sugar
> Lemon wedges and fresh parsley sprigs for garnish

Remove the heads from the herrings, clean, gut and bone them. Wash the herrings and pat them thoroughly dry. Put the breadcrumbs, parsley, lemon juice and lemon rind in a basin; season lightly with salt and freshly ground black pepper. Melt the butter and stir into the breadcrumbs to bind the mixture, which should now be moist, but crumbly. Stuff the herrings with the breadcrumb mixture, and if necessary secure them with wooden cocktail sticks. Slash the skins crossways two or three times on each side; brush the herrings with oil and wrap each in foil. Put the herrings in a well-buttered deep baking dish; cover with lightly buttered greaseproof paper and bake in the centre of a pre-heated oven at 200°C/400°F/Gas Mark 6 for 35-40 minutes.

For the sauce, melt 25g/1oz of the butter in a pan; stir in the flour and cook for 1 minute. Gradually stir in the milk, beating well until the sauce is quite smooth. Bring to the boil and simmer for 2-3 minutes; season with salt and pepper. Blend the mustard powder with the vinegar and stir into the sauce; add the sugar. Check seasoning and stir in the remaining butter.

Transfer the baked herrings to a hot serving dish and garnish with wedges of lemon and sprigs of parsley. Serve the mustard sauce separately.

GREAT YARMOUTH, FISH MARKET c1900 G56503

QUIZ ANSWERS

1. The classic book 'Black Beauty' was written by Anna Sewell, who was born in Great Yarmouth in 1820 in a house on Church Plain, and lived at Old Catton, now part of Norwich, from 1866 until her death in 1878. 'Black Beauty' was written to protest against cruelty to horses, and has sold around 40 million copies since it was published in 1877. Anna Sewell is remembered in Norwich in the name of Sewell Park, Sewell Road, and the Sewell Barn Theatre in the grounds of Sewell Park College.

2. The Great Yarmouth MP Miles Corbet supported Parliament in the Civil War, and was one of the signatories to Charles I's death warrant in 1649. When Charles II was restored to the throne in 1660, he fled abroad. He was brought back to stand trial, condemned for high treason, and suffered the ghastly death of being hanged, drawn and quartered.

3. Sir Robert Walpole (1676-1745) was also the MP for King's Lynn for 40 years.

4. Samson is on the left hand side of the photograph on page 47, holding a lamb, and Hercules is on the right, with a lion's skin around his waist.

5. Named after the River Stiff, the Norfolk village of Stiffkey is famous for its 'Stookey (or Stewkey) Blues' – blue-shelled Norfolk cockles.

6. 'Quanting' is a word used on the Norfolk Broads for the action of propelling a boat with a long pole – seen on page 7.

7. 'The Babes in the Wood' is believed to be based on a true story from 16th-century Norfolk, when two children were left orphaned. Their wicked uncle (said to have lived at Griston Hall) ordered his men to take the children into Wayland Wood south of Watton and murder them, so he could claim their inheritance. However, the men could not bring themselves to kill the children, but abandoned them in the wood, where they soon died. Their ghosts are said to haunt the wood, which was known as Wailing Wood in the past. The Babes in the Wood are depicted on the village signs for both Griston and Watton.

8. Grimes' Graves is an ancient flint mine from the late Neolithic period. Ancient man used Norfolk's rich flint deposits for making flint-knapped tools and axes. Flint was mined here on a large scale over 5,000 years ago, and the pits, shafts and quarries of the prehistoric workings can still be seen. The Anglo-Saxons named them after their god Grim, calling them 'Grim's quarries', or 'the Devil's holes'. The mines are open to visitors, who can descend by ladder into an excavated mine shaft.

9. The Victorians called her Boadicea, but she is now known as Boudicca (or Boudica), queen of the Iceni tribe, whose territory covered Norfolk. She led a rising against the Romans around AD60, and her forces sacked and burned London before being defeated.

10. 'Staithe' means a landing place, ie from a river or a stretch of water in the Broads.

**GREAT YARMOUTH,
REGENT ROAD
1896** 37959v

FRANCIS FRITH

PIONEER VICTORIAN PHOTOGRAPHER

Francis Frith, founder of the world-famous photographic archive, was a complex and multi-talented man. A devout Quaker and a highly successful Victorian businessman, he was philosophical by nature and pioneering in outlook. By 1855 he had already established a wholesale grocery business in Liverpool, and sold it for the astonishing sum of £200,000, which is the equivalent today of over £15,000,000. Now in his thirties, and captivated by the new science of photography, Frith set out on a series of pioneering journeys up the Nile and to the Near East.

INTRIGUE AND EXPLORATION

He was the first photographer to venture beyond the sixth cataract of the Nile. Africa was still the mysterious 'Dark Continent', and Stanley and Livingstone's historic meeting was a decade into the future. The conditions for picture taking confound belief. He laboured for hours in his wicker dark-room in the sweltering heat of the desert, while the volatile chemicals fizzed dangerously in their trays. Back in London he exhibited his photographs and was 'rapturously cheered' by members of the Royal Society. His reputation as a photographer was made overnight.

VENTURE OF A LIFE-TIME

By the 1870s the railways had threaded their way across the country, and Bank Holidays and half-day Saturdays had been made obligatory by Act of Parliament. All of a sudden the working man and his family were able to enjoy days out, take holidays, and see a little more of the world.

With typical business acumen, Francis Frith foresaw that these new tourists would enjoy having souvenirs to commemorate their days out. For the next thirty years he travelled the country by train and by pony and trap, producing fine photographs of seaside resorts and beauty spots that were keenly bought by millions of Victorians. These prints were painstakingly pasted into family albums and pored over during the dark nights of winter, rekindling precious memories of summer excursions. Frith's studio was soon supplying retail shops all over the country, and by 1890 F Frith & Co had become the greatest specialist photographic publishing company in the world, with over 2,000 sales outlets, and pioneered the picture postcard.

FRANCIS FRITH'S LEGACY

Francis Frith had died in 1898 at his villa in Cannes, his great project still growing. By 1970 the archive he created contained over a third of a million pictures showing 7,000 British towns and villages.

Frith's legacy to us today is of immense significance and value, for the magnificent archive of evocative photographs he created provides a unique record of change in the cities, towns and villages throughout Britain over a century and more. Frith and his fellow studio photographers revisited locations many times down the years to update their views, compiling for us an enthralling and colourful pageant of British life and character.

We are fortunate that Frith was dedicated to recording the minutiae of everyday life. For it is this sheer wealth of visual data, the painstaking chronicle of changes in dress, transport, street layouts, buildings, housing and landscape that captivates us so much today, offering us a powerful link with the past and with the lives of our ancestors.

Computers have now made it possible for Frith's many thousands of images to be accessed almost instantly. The archive offers every one of us an opportunity to examine the places where we and our families have lived and worked down the years. Its images, depicting our shared past, are now bringing pleasure and enlightenment to millions around the world a century and more after his death.

For further information visit: www.francisfrith.com

INTERIOR DECORATION

Frith's photographs can be seen framed and as giant wall murals in thousands of pubs, restaurants, hotels, banks, retail stores and other public buildings throughout Britain. These provide interesting and attractive décor, generating strong local interest and acting as a powerful reminder of gentler days in our increasingly busy and frenetic world.

FRITH PRODUCTS

All Frith photographs are available as prints and posters in a variety of different sizes and styles. In the UK we also offer a range of other gift and stationery products illustrated with Frith photographs, although many of these are not available for delivery outside the UK – see our web site for more information on the products available for delivery in your country.

THE INTERNET

Over 100,000 photographs of Britain can be viewed and purchased on the Frith web site. The web site also includes memories and reminiscences contributed by our customers, who have personal knowledge of localities and of the people and properties depicted in Frith photographs. If you wish to learn more about a specific town or village you may find these reminiscences fascinating to browse. Why not add your own comments if you think they would be of interest to others? See **www.francisfrith.com**

PLEASE HELP US BRING FRITH'S PHOTOGRAPHS TO LIFE

Our authors do their best to recount the history of the places they write about. They give insights into how particular towns and villages developed, they describe the architecture of streets and buildings, and they discuss the lives of famous people who lived there. But however knowledgeable our authors are, the story they tell is necessarily incomplete.

Frith's photographs are so much more than plain historical documents. They are living proofs of the flow of human life down the generations. They show real people at real moments in history; and each of those people is the son or daughter of someone, the brother or sister, aunt or uncle, grandfather or grandmother of someone else. All of them lived, worked and played in the streets depicted in Frith's photographs.

We would be grateful if you would give us your insights into the places shown in our photographs: the streets and buildings, the shops, businesses and industries. Post your memories of life in those streets on the Frith website: what it was like growing up there, who ran the local shop and what shopping was like years ago; if your workplace is shown tell us about your working day and what the building is used for now. Read other visitors' memories and reconnect with your shared local history and heritage. With your help more and more Frith photographs can be brought to life, and vital memories preserved for posterity, and for the benefit of historians in the future.

Wherever possible, we will try to include some of your comments in future editions of our books. Moreover, if you spot errors in dates, titles or other facts, please let us know, because our archive records are not always completely accurate—they rely on 140 years of human endeavour and hand-compiled records. You can email us using the contact form on the website.

Thank you!

For further information, trade, or author enquiries
please contact us at the address below:

**The Francis Frith Collection, Unit 6, Oakley Business Park,
Wylye Road, Dinton, Wiltshire SP3 5EU.**
Tel: +44 (0)1722 716 376 Fax: +44 (0)1722 716 881
e-mail: sales@francisfrith.co.uk **www.francisfrith.com**